I0142280

# Don't Laugh at Me!

Written and illustrated by Greg Armstrong

Special thanks to Christie Wolenski for enhancing the delivery of Buddy's heartfelt message to the child.

## Buddy's World AND FRIENDS

© 2012 Buddy's World and Friends. All rights reserved.

www.buddysworldandfriends.com

Buddy used to
like school.

OAKLAND BUDDY

CHARGER BUDDY

Buddy of Anaheim

BUDDY

Page 2

Buddy's mom doesn't know that he hates school now.

# Page 4

His mom gets mad when
he doesn't want to go
to school.

OAKLAND BUDDY

CHARGER BUDDY

Buddy of Anaheim

Buddy tries to act like he's sick so his mom won't get mad.

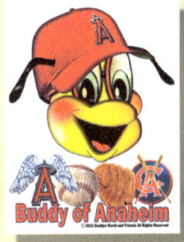

But Buddy's mom knows
he's not sick.

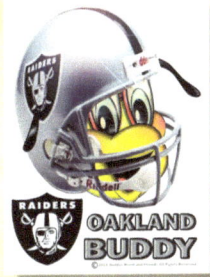

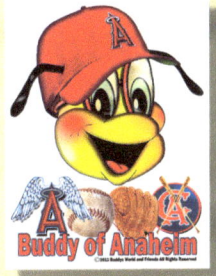

Buddy is afraid of being laughed at in school.

He tells his mom about
the kids at school
laughing at him
and it makes him cry.

Buddy's mom thinks
about girls who laughed
at her when she was
Buddy's age.
This makes her sad, too.

Buddy thinks about the
mean boy at school
and feels very sad.

They both forget they are
sad and start to dance
and sing.

Buddy tries to cheer up
his mom by telling her
a joke. He forgets he
is sad, too.

Buddy knows he is loved.
Buddy is in safe hands by
people who love him.

Kids, when you feel sad,
color my picture!

# BULLYING HURTS !

©2012 Buddys World and Friends All Rights Reserved

Special thanks to Christie Wolenski for enhancing the delivery of Buddy's heartfelt message to the child.

www.ingramcontent.com/pod-product-compliance
Lightning Source LLC
LaVergne TN
LVHW010024070426
835508LV00001B/45